Flowers of my heart
(*Poetry*)

By:
Marguba Abdurazokova

© Taemeer Publications LLC
Flowers of my heart *(Poetry)*
by: Marguba Abdurazokova
Edition: August '2023
Publisher:
Taemeer Publications LLC (Michigan, USA / Hyderabad, India)

© Taemeer Publications

Book	:	Flowers of my heart *(Poetry)*
Author	:	Marguba Abdurazokova
Publisher	:	Taemeer Publications
Year	:	'2023
Pages	:	40
Title Design	:	*Taemeer Web Design*

Table of Content

1	Be patient	5
2	Forgive me, mother	7
3	I miss my real friend	9
4	You are alive in my heart	11
5	My soul	12
6	You are my dream	14
7	Our love is forever	15
8	The flag of Uzbekistan	17
9	Shine	18
10	Love is dead in my heart	20
11	Flowers are for me	21
12	Ahmad Yassaviy	23
13	I will find my way	25
14	Zulfiya	26
15	Real beauty	27
16	A melody of life	29
17	Tears of baby	31
18	Uzbekistan is home to all nations	32
19	Rain	34
20	Diamonds	35
21	Don't say goodbye	37
22	Do not give up!	38

Marguba Abdurazokova is a new poetess from Uzbekistan. She is an active member of different organizations, such as The "Universe" free volunteering movement, The "Iqra" Foundation of Pakistan, Asih Sasami Indonesia Global Writers, and The Egyptian international organization "Creativity Forum for Arts, Cultures, and Peace". Her poems had published in The Turkish magazine "Güncel Sanat", The Azerbaijani newspaper "Türküstan", "She'riy guldasta" ("Poetic Bouquet") Anthology, "Turkish Uzbek Voice 2", "Leader Girls Lead the World", "The most successful girls of Uzbekistan", "Talented Voices of Uzbekistan", Turkish and American International Anthology and she has poetic books, such as "Gulbahor" and "The Universe of Uzbekistan". She has participated in an international festival "World in Uzbekistan International Literary Festival".

1
Be patient

In a world that rushes and races on,
Amidst the chaos, where dreams are drawn,
A virtue so rare, yet profoundly profound,
Is the art of patience, a gem to be found?

Like a tranquil river that calmly flows,
Patience weaves serenity, as life goes,
It's a gentle whisper in a world of noise,
Guiding us through trials and tough choices.

With eyes that see beyond the present storm,
Patience holds the key to hearts forlorn,
For in its embrace, we find solace and peace,
A refuge where troubled minds can release.

In nature's canvas, seasons paint with grace,
A masterful display of time's slow embrace,
For buds bloom not at once, but in their stead,
Patience paints each petal, where beauty spread.

In love's delicate dance, patience finds its place,
Nurturing affection with a tender embrace,
Two souls entwining, like vines on a wall,
Patience gives love roots, so it will not fall.

When challenges towers and mountains seem tall,
Patience whispers courage, to stand and not fall,
With perseverance's might and hope as its creed,
Patience turns mountains into mere mustard seeds.

In learning's journey, like a humble seed,
Patience nurtures wisdom from a tiny bead,
With every step, knowledge begins to bloom,
In the fertile fields where patience looms.

Though the world spins fast, let's slow our gait,
Embrace the grace of patience, never belate,
For in its embrace, we find strength to endure,
Life's uncertain paths are steadfast and pure.

So, let patience be a beacon, a guiding light,
Illuminating our way through the darkest night,
In this hurried world, let's cherish this art,
A gift that brings hope and peace to every heart.

2
Forgive me, mother

In the depths of time's unyielding flow,
I seek the solace I used to know,
Within the haven of your loving embrace,
A tender warmth, a sacred space.

Yet, I faltered on my path's endeavor,
And caused your heart profound displeasure.
Oh, forgive me, Mother, for my mistakes,
For every tear that my soul aches.

In youth's folly, I wandered astray,
Ignoring wisdom's whispered say.
In haste, I cast my dreams aside,
Blinded by foolishness and pride.

But now, the veil of ignorance is torn,
And in retrospection, I am forlorn,
For I comprehend the pain I caused,
The wounds inflicted, the trust paused.

I yearn to turn back the hands of time,
To amend my errors, to make amends prime.
But in humility, I come to you,
With a heart contrite, and words anew.

I seek no pardon without remorse,
No fleeting plea, a hollow discourse.
My plea for forgiveness is sincere,
To heal the bond, bring love near.

In the tapestry of life's grand art,
A mother's love plays a vital part.
Your compassion, a boundless sea,
Forgiveness is a gift that sets me free.

Through the darkest storms that transpire,
Your love remains, a steady fire,
Guiding me to a place of grace,
A sanctuary, a warm embrace.

So, forgive me, Mother, I implore,
May your kindness wash me ashore,
In your embrace, let the healing start,
A second chance, a brand-new start.

3
I miss my real friend

A true friend was lost, yet memories remain,
In every whispered breeze and falling rain.

I miss you, oh dear friend, like stars miss the night,
Your laughter and warmth, are like a guiding light.
Through ups and downs, we stood side by side,
In every storm and joy, you were my guide.

Your genuine smile, like sunshine in my soul,
With you, I was complete, I felt whole.
We shared our dreams, our fears, our pain,
In your embrace, I found solace again.

In distant lands, our paths took flight,
Time and distance created this divide.
But no distance can erase the bond we share,
For true friendship, beyond miles, can dare.

I miss you, my real friend, more than words can say,
In my thoughts and dreams, you still hold sway.
Though life's currents may pull us apart,
Know that you reside within my heart.

When life's burdens weigh heavy on my chest,
I yearn for the comfort of your presence's crest.
With you, I could be my authentic self,
A treasure, a gift, like a rare book on the shelf.

So here's to the memories, the laughter, the tears,
To the moments we cherished throughout the years.
Though I miss you deeply, let our friendship be,
A beacon of love, eternally free.

And when the stars align, and our paths intertwine,
I know, my real friend, everything will be fine.
Until that day, I'll cherish you from afar,
True friends are forever, no matter how far.

4
You are alive in my heart

In the depths of my being, a spark ignites,
A flame that burns, a guiding light,
For in my heart, you are alive,
A cherished presence that will never die.

Through the trials and tempest's gale,
Your memory stands, it shall not pale,
For every beat, your name does start,
An echo of love, deep in my heart.

The days may pass, and years may go,
Yet your essence blooms, a steady glow,
In the tapestry of life, you are a part of,
An eternal connection, deep in my heart.

Like a gentle breeze, your laughter's grace,
It brings warmth and comfort, a sweet embrace,
In every joy, in moments of strife,
You dwell within me, enriching my life.

Through the darkest hours, you're my guide,
A constant presence, a soothing tide,
Your love's a beacon, a radiant art,
A treasured gift, alive in my heart.

Though distance may stand, we're not apart,
For you're woven in the fabric of my heart,
In the symphony of memories, we'll never part,
Forever entwined, you are alive in my heart.

5
My soul

In the realm where shadows dance,
Where dreams and thoughts find their chance,
Resides a being, ethereal, whole,
A tapestry woven, your precious soul.

A symphony of hues, emotions untold,
A timeless story, in you, it unfolds.
In depths uncharted, a mystic sea,
A soul's journey, boundless and free.

Through joys and tears, it finds its way,
Through darkest nights and brightest days.
A beacon of light, it seeks to find,
The purpose and meaning g, intertwined.

In moments of doubt, it finds its might,
In tender love, it taits flight.
A mirror reflecting the inner core,
A treasure trove, an endless store.

It weathers storms and seeks light,
A phoenix is rising, bold and bright.
With scars that tell tales of battles fought,
Yet, the purest love, it still has brought.

In shadows' grasp, it may briefly sway,
But hope and strength shall light the way.
For in your soul, resilience thrives,
A spark of eternity, it derives.

Embrace the dance, both light and shade,
For every part, a role is well-played.
Your soul, a masterpiece to behold,
A journey of wonder, yet untold.

6
You are my dream

In twilight's soft embrace, you gleam,
A vision fair, my cherished theme,
A wondrous world where stars align,
You are my dream, forever mine.

In slumber's realm, we intertwine,
Bound by love's ethereal twine,
In dreamscape dance, we take flight,
You are my dream, my guiding light.

Like moonlit whispers, soft and sweet,
Your presence makes my heart complete,
Through shadows dark or skies agleam,
You are my dream, my soul's esteem.

Your laughter rings like a melody,
A symphony of serenity,
In reverie, I feel the gleam,
You are my dream, my cherished theme.

Through distant realms, our spirits soar,
Where fantasies, enchantments pour,
In every thought, a world redeemed,
You are my dream, the one I've dreamed of.

Though the morning sun may bring the day,
In dreams, our love will never sway,
For in my heart, you reign supreme,
You are my dream, my endless dream.

7
Our love is forever

Through starlit nights and sunlit days,
Our hearts embrace in endless ways,
A symphony of love's sweet tune,
We'll dance beneath both sun and moon.

In every moment, we'll ignite,
With passion's flame, a glowing light,
An endless blaze, forever bright,
Guiding us through the darkest night.

Like ancient trees, our roots entwine,
In depths of love, we both align,
With every breath, a sacred vow,
To cherish, honor, here and now.

Through joy and tears, hand in hand,
Together, strong, we'll firmly stand,
And when the storms of life draw near,
Love's fortress strong will conquer fear.

As seasons change, and years advance,
Our love will grow, take every chance,
To blossom like a fragrant flower,
Enduring, lasting, love's true power.

No boundaries, no limits set,
Our love, a bond they can't forget,
For in this universe so vast,
Our love is endless, unsurpassed.

So, let time's sands keep slipping through,
As long as I have love for you,
Eternity is ours to serve,
Forevermore, our love is forever.

8
The flag of Uzbekistan

In the azure skies of Uzbekistan's land,
A banner of pride unfurls, oh so grand.
Its colors, like a dream, they soar and rise,
A symphony of hues, that mesmerize.

A field of blue, the canvas of the sky,
A symbol of hope that soars up high.
For unity and peace, it stands tall,
Embracing every heart, both big and small.

A crescent moon, shining bright and clear,
A beacon of hope dispelling fear.
It guides the nation through each darkest night,
With gleaming promise, steadfast light.

And next to it, a star of purest white,
Reflecting dreams, and ambitions, and taking flight.
In unity, its five points do entwine,
The strength of heritage, a bond divine.

Like ancient echoes from the past, they call,
History is woven, and shared by all.
The flag of Uzbekistan, a timeless thread,
Through trials and triumphs, it has led.

With every flutter, a story's told,
Of a nation brave, of tales of old.
In colors bold, a future yet to be,
The Uzbekistan flag waves are proud and free.

9
Shine

A brilliance born of cosmic dance,
In galaxies and realms askance,
From distant suns to earthly streams,
Shine's woven in life's vibrant seams.

Upon the ocean's gleaming crest,
A sparkling trail, an invitation's quest,
To sail beyond the horizon's bend,
Where shine and mystery both transcend.

In forests deep, where shadows hide,
A shaft of light breaks through, abides,
On emerald leaves, it gently gleams,
A lustrous touch, a nature's dream.

From tender smiles on newborn's faces,
To weathered hands that time embrace,
In every heart and soul entwined,
Shine's spark ignites, a love defined.

Yet shine's not just in days of cheer,
It flickers brightly through the darkest fear,
For in the depths, we find our strength,
To rise, rebuild, and go to lengths.

In acts of kindness, pure and true,
In words that lift, in deeds we do,
Shine's found in moments big or small,
A guiding light through life's enthralling.

So let us cherish, never spurn,
The gift of shine, in each in turn,
Embrace the glow that's ours to share,
A beacon bright, for all to bear.

10
Love is dead in my heart

In the depths of my soul, darkness lies,
Where once a flame of love burned bright,
But now, that fire has grown cold and died,
And all that's left is an endless night.

The laughter we shared, the joy we knew,
Now lost in the shadows of the past,
Once tender words, now bitter and untrue,
Love's beauty faded, its spell now cast.

No more the tender touch, the sweet embrace,
The warmth that once defined our connection,
Replaced by emptiness and love's cold space,
Leaving only sorrow and reflection.

In this heart of mine, love's flame has ceased,
A shattered dream, a love once inspired,
Now all that's left is pain and heartache, increased,
And the memories of love have now expired.

But though the embers of love may be gone,
Within the darkness, hope can still be found,
For hearts can heal and find a new dawn,
With time and care, love can be unbound.

So, though love may be dead in my heart,
I'll hold onto hope as the days go by,
For someday, a new love may impart,
And once again, my heart will soar high.

11
Flowers are for me

In gardens kissed by a gentle breeze,
Where sunbeams weave a golden frieze,
I wander through a realm of glee,
Where flowers bloom, and dreams run free.

Their petals soft like whispered sighs,
In hues that paint the vibrant skies,
Each blossom tells a tale untold,
Of love, of hope, of secrets bold.

The rose, adorned with crimson dress,
A symbol of love's sweet caress,
Its thorns remind me of passion's fire,
That burns with every heart's desire.

The lily dons pure attire,
A beacon in the night's empire,
Its fragrance, like a soothing balm,
In troubled hearts brings newfound calm.

The daisy in its innocence,
A symbol of sweet recompense,
With every petal, loves me, loves me not,
A playful game of fate, unsought.

Tulips tall in rainbow hues,
A joyful dance, a vibrant muse,
They sway beneath the azure dome,
In gardens, they have found their home.

The lavender, a fragrant spell,
Its purple blooms, a tale to tell,
Of peaceful nights and tranquil dreams,
Where stardust falls in silver streams.

With every bloom that graces me,
A symphony of colors I see,
They speak of life's divine embrace,
And nature's awe-inspiring grace.

Flowers are for me, a gift divine,
A tapestry of life's design,
In their beauty, I find my way,
A haven in the chaos' fray.

So let me walk through fields of flowers,
And lose myself for timeless hours,
For in their presence, I'm set free,
Flowers are for me, and I for thee.

12
Ahmad Yassaviy

In the realm of mystic tales, a sage did rise,
Ahmad Yassaviy, a soul that touched the skies.
Born amidst the steppes, where wild winds blow,
His heart was ablaze, with divine love aglow.

A poet's pen, he wielded with grace,
Unraveling truths in each written trace.
In words, he wove a tapestry of light,
Guiding lost souls through the darkest night.

With verses like stars, his wisdom shone,
A beacon of hope for hearts forlorn.
His thoughts are like rivers, flowing free,
Connecting souls in unity.

A Sufi saint, with an inner fire,
Kindling souls with pure desire.
Through love, he found the path within,
To reach the essence, to shed the skin.

The dervishes danced to rhythms unseen,
Whirling like galaxies in a cosmic dream.
In the Sama's trance, they found release,
The divine ecstasy, the ultimate peace.

His teachings echoed through the ages,
Resonating still on history's pages.
In the caravanserai of the heart,
He taught that love transcends all art.

Ahmad Yassaviy, a mystic so divine,
An inspiration for hearts to align.
In his legacy, we find our way,
To embrace the light and keep the darkness at bay.

13
I will find my way

In the depths of the darkest night, I'll stray,
Through shadows and doubts, I'll find my way.
Amidst the whispers of uncertainty's sway,
I'll seek the stars to light my pathway.

In mazes of fear, I won't lose sight,
I'll forge ahead, like a beacon's might.
For every stumble, a lesson's flight,
I'll rise with hope, my heart alight.

Through treacherous storms that rage and roar,
I'll brace the tempests, endure and soar.
With every challenge, I'll learn to soar,
In the face of adversity, I'll explore.

The trials may test my resolve to stay,
Yet, I'll persevere, I'll not dismay.
With the strength within, I'll seize the day,
My spirit is unyielding, come what may.

Though the journey's length, I can't foresee,
I'll trust the path, where it leads me.
Each step forward, a destiny decree,
In the realm of dreams, I'll wander free.

For destiny calls, an unwritten play,
I'll embrace the unknown without delay.
Through the highs and lows, come what may,
I'll find my way, day by day.

14
Zulfiya

In fields of knowledge, she excelled,
The tales of wisdom she would tell,
A beacon bright, a guiding ray,
Empowering others on their way.

A friend to hearts that sought her aid,
Her empathy, a soothing shade,
In Zulfiya's arms, burdens eased,
Her comfort was like a gentle breeze.

Yet, with her tender heart so pure,
She braved the storms that would endure,
For life, though kind, is not all ease,
Yet Zulfiya's spirit did not cease.

Her legacy, a cherished gift,
A tapestry of souls uplifted,
In every life she touched, she'd live,
A spark of love she'd surely give.

So let us raise our voices high,
In praise of her across the sky,
For Zulfiya, a soul so bright,
Forever in our hearts, alight.

15
Real beauty

In realms where beauty's truth resides,
Beyond mere looks and shallow tides,
Where hearts are seen and souls set free,
There blooms a beauty, pure decree.

It's not confined to skin or eye,
But dwells in depths that words can't tie,
A radiance that lights the core,
A beauty, like the ocean's roar.

It graces kindness in its sway,
In gentle deeds, it finds its way,
A smile that warms a troubled mind,
A hand that's there, to help, to bind.

True beauty's not a perfect form,
But lives in flaws that we adorn,
For scars and marks, they tell a tale,
Of strength and grace that can't assail.

In laughter's dance, it takes its flight,
A melody of sheer delight,
It weaves through tears, like rain's embrace,
And gives the heart a sacred space.

Real beauty's found in empathy,
In feeling others' agony,
To lift them when shadows fall,
To hear their voice, to heed their call.

It thrives in love, both fierce and kind,
In selflessness, the heart aligned,
A love that's boundless, infinite,
A guiding star through the darkest night.

The mirror shows but just one side,
For inner beauty can't be tied,
It shines from depths within the soul,
A precious gem that makes us whole.

So let us seek, with open eyes,
This beauty, real, that never dies,
Embrace the hearts that beat as one,
For there, true beauty has begun.

16
A melody of life

In the hush of twilight's golden gleam,
A melody of life begins to dream,
Whispers of nature's tender call,
In every heartbeat, it denthrallhral.

The gentle rustle of leaves in the breeze,
Plays a symphony among the trees,
A cadence of seasons, ebb and flow,
In this wondrous journey, we bestow.

Through sunlit days and moonlit nights,
The melody of life takes to new heights,
In joyous laughter and tears that fall,
We dance to the rhythm of it all.

When shadows cast their solemn grace,
And trials test our mortal space,
Still, the melody hums, steadfast and true,
Guiding our steps as we push through.

With each dawn's chorus, we find hope,
In each dusk's serenade, we learn to cope,
For life's song, a tapestry finely spun,
With threads of love, we are all bound as one.

From the cradle's lullaby to life's final breath,
The melody of existence knows no death,
It carries on through ages untold,
An eternal refrain that shall never fold.

Embrace this harmony, let your spirit fly,
Like a soaring eagle in the boundless sky,
For in this symphony of joy and strife,
We find the essence—the melody of life.

17
Tears of baby

In the cradle of innocence, a miracle's born,
A tiny being, fresh as the morn,
Blessed with eyes of wonder and grace,
A new life to cherish, hold and embrace.

The world is a canvas, unknown and bright,
With tears and laughter, day and night,
And as the stars twinkle in the vast sky above,
The tears of a baby convey their love.

In cries that echo through the quiet night,
Their tears speak a language, pure and bright,
A prism of emotion, each teardrop a hue,
Painting emotions, every shade so true.

The tears of a baby, a symphony of the heart,
A melody of feelings, a masterpiece of art,
For in those droplets, as they trickle down,
A world of dreams and hopes are found.

With each tear shed, a story unfolds,
Of fears and joys, yet to be told,
They bond us together, human and near,
Washing away sorrow, bringing us cheer.

In tears, they find solace and release,
Their tiny souls, seeking inner peace,
A river of innocence, a stream of grace,
Their tears embrace us, love's warm embrace.

18
Uzbekistan is home to all nations

In Uzbekistan's embrace, diversity thrives,
A land where countless cultures unite,
From distant corners, hearts arrive,
To share in its welcoming light.

Oh, Uzbekistan, the land of grace,
Where colors blend in harmony's dance,
In every smile, in every face,
A tapestry of cultures enhances.

In Samarkand's ancient city walls,
Silk Road tales weave through the air,
Where traders' echoes softly call,
And history's whispers linger there.

Tashkent, a bustling modern heart,
With open arms, it warmly greets,
Embracing all, it plays its part,
In a symphony of diverse beats.

The nomad's spirit roams the steppe,
As echoes of yurts dot the plains,
In unity, their bonds are kept,
While traditional melodies sustain.

In Fergana's valleys, colors bloom,
Like a garden of humanity,
Bound by love, not borders' gloom,
Fostering peace and unity.

From Karakalpakstan to Khorezm's land,
And Pamirs where the mountains soar,
Each region's heritage, grand,
A cherished treasure to explore.

Through markets bustling with spices and sounds,
And artisan crafts rich and rare,
Every culture here is crowned,
With admiration and mutual care.
Uzbekistan, a cradle of civilization's might,
Nurturing seeds from every clime,
In your embrace, day turns to night,
As love transcends the bounds of time.

19
Rain

In the hush of twilight's embrace, a dance begins to play,
As the heavens weep in gentle grace, a melody they sway.
The sky's tears fall from heights above, a symphony of sighs,
A rhythmic chorus, filled with love, as raindrops touch our eyes.

A lullaby of nature's soul, where dreams and memories meet,
In every drop, a story's told, a journey bittersweet.
The rooftops sing the rivers hum, the leaves a gentle thrum,
Each raindrop plays a part, as one, in this wet ballet of the sun.

The parched earth welcomes tenderly, each droplet's soft caress,
A kiss from clouds so heavenly, a union to impress.
The petals of a flower bloom, in vibrant colors they ignite,
A canvas painted by the gloom, a masterpiece of night.

The children laugh and run outside, their laughter fills the air,
They dance beneath the stormy tide, without a single care.
Splashing puddles, faces bright, in innocent delight,
With every drop, a pure delight, they revel in the night.

The city streets are washed anew, cleansed of dust and grime,
Reflecting skies of deepest blue, in rain's embrace, they chime.
Through neon lights, the raindrops gleam, like diamonds in the dark,
A mesmerizing, shimmering dream, the city's beating heart.

The forest whispers secrets old, beneath the gentle rain,
An ancient tale of life untold, reborn again and again.
The creatures seek their cozy nooks, protected from the storm,
They find solace in nature's books, their spirits are safe and warm.

20
Diamonds

In the realm of words, my gems do gleam,
A treasure trove of dreams, it would seem,
For within the lines, my heart's design,
My poems are diamonds, radiant and fine.

Each verse a facet polished bright,
Reflecting on feelings, thoughts taking flight,
With every syllable, a gemstone's hue,
In kaleidoscope colors, they shine through.

Emotions cut, faceted clear,
In rhymes and rhythms, they appear,
A symphony of words, a poet's delight,
My gems of expression, day and night.

Some are diamonds, pure and rare,
Sparkling with joy, beyond compare,
Others, deep sapphires, profound and blue,
Expressing sorrows, known to few.

Emeralds of hope, in the lush green array,
Glimmers of faith, in times of dismay,
Ruby verses, passion's fire unfurled,
Igniting the soul, in a poetic world.

Opals of laughter, with humor entwined,
Topaz truths, with wisdom aligned,
Amidst this treasure trove, a crown,
A diamond tiara, to call my own.

For my poems are my diamonds, you see,
A precious gift, bestowed on me,
They light the darkness, they bring delight,
My eternal gems, in ink I write.

21
Don't say goodbye

In the twilight's embrace, we'll find solace together,
Like shooting stars, our paths may cross, forever.
Don't say goodbye, for in the stars we're entwined,
In the universe's grand design, love is undefined.

The whispers of the wind will carry our dreams,
Across vast oceans, through moonlit streams.
Though distance may stretch and time may fly,
Our hearts shall remain connected, soaring high.

Embrace the laughter and cherish each tear,
For in every experience, our souls draw near.
Life's a tapestry, woven with threads of delight,
Don't say goodbye; let love's flame burn bright.

The melodies we shared will echo through time,
A symphony of emotions, a rhythm sublime.
Even in the darkest night, you're not alone,
For within our hearts, a sacred bond is sown.

So let the sunsets kiss the horizons with grace,
As we dance in the moon's soft, silvery embrace.
With each passing day, our spirits will unify,
In the dance of existence, we'll never say goodbye.

In the cosmic dance of life, we find our place,
Embracing love's beauty, weaving our embrace.
Though paths may diverge, and tears may fall like rain,
Our souls entwined, forever to remain.

So, let us not utter those sorrowful words,
For in each other's hearts, we'll always be heard.
In the tapestry of life, where our spirits fly,
Let's bid farewell to goodbyes and never say goodbye.

22
Do not give up!

In shadows cast upon the path, where darkness may confound,
A weary heart with heavy steps, in solitude, is bound.
Yet, in the depths of trials faced, where hope may seem undone,
Lies the strength to persevere, to rise and greet the sun.

Don't give up, oh steadfast soul, when storms begin to brew,
For every tempest that arrives, shall surely pass anew.
Though thunder roars and lightning strikes, and doubts attempt to creep,
A resolute spirit stands tall, while others may retreat.

In every valley's shadowed veil, where doubts obscure the light,
Remember, strength lies deep within, obscured but burning bright.
When tears like raindrops gently fall, and skies are draped in gray,
Find solace in the truth proclaimed, that this too shall decay.

The road ahead may twist and turn, and obstacles abound,
Yet in the face of trials fierce, determination's found.
Each step you take is a testament, your will remains unbowed,
Through trials and tribulations faced, your spirit's strength avowed.

When failures cast their somber shroud, and dreams seem far away,
Recall that even stars are born amidst the darkest fray.
Embrace each scar and battle wound, they tell a tale of grit,
For strength is forged in fires of doubt, and courage is found in it.

Don't give up, oh valiant heart, though weary is your tread,
A seed of hope lies deep within, in time, it will be fed.
With each new dawn that breaks the night, a chance to start anew,
To gather strength and rise again, the sky's the canvas you pursue.

In moments when you feel alone, with burdens hard to bear,
Remember, you are not defined by troubles or despair.
With every step, you're forging on, a warrior through and through,
For in the depths of every soul, lies strength that will renew.

So, heed the call of resilience, and let it be your guide,
With courage as your compass true, in you, the stars reside.
Don't give up, oh radiant soul, embrace the journey's call,
For in the tapestry of life, you are the bravest thread of all.

Printed in the USA
CPSIA information can be obtained
at www.ICGtesting.com
LVHW011112210923
758644LV00012B/358